FLORAL DESIGNS

Coloring Book

Flower Patterns & Mandalas for Relaxation

Pepper Kaufman

ISBN: 978-1511952439

Printed in the United States of America.

NOTES

Those who incorporate creative methods to relieve stress in their lives are often far happier and healthier than those who don't. Meditation, or some form of introspective balancing, can help greatly. It takes time, effort, and true commitment to develop such skills, right? Well, not if you introduce coloring into your life. It isn't necessarily about creating a work of art. It's about reducing stress, relaxing, enhancing your creativity, focusing on your center, improving your chi, improving your health… and having tons of fun in the process! Sometimes, true joy comes from the simplest actions. Spend just a few minutes a day coloring these floral patterns and mandala designs. It may not change your life, but it can certainly help you feel more focused, relaxed and centered. Of course, once you start, you most likely won't want to stop. Enjoy!

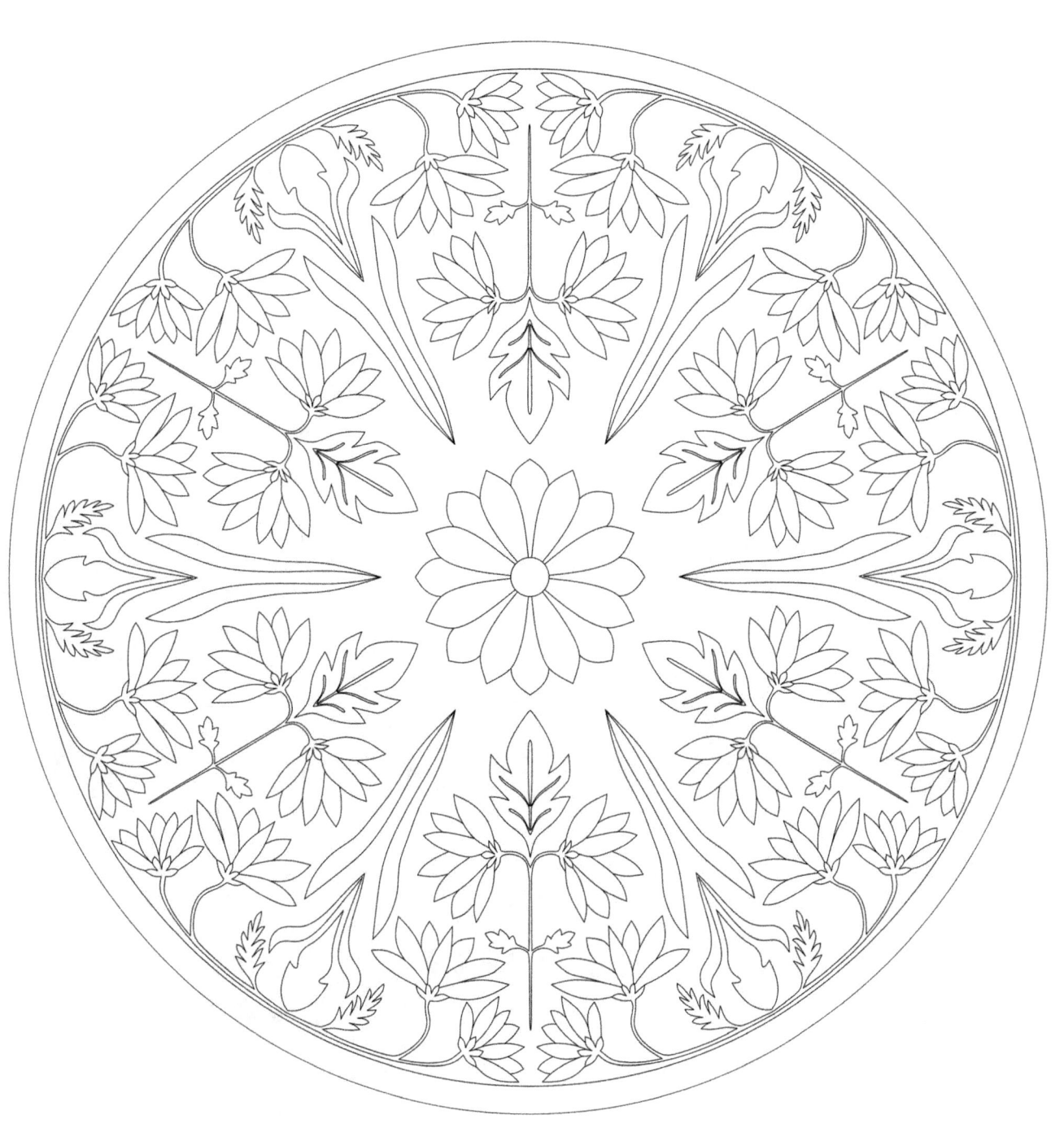

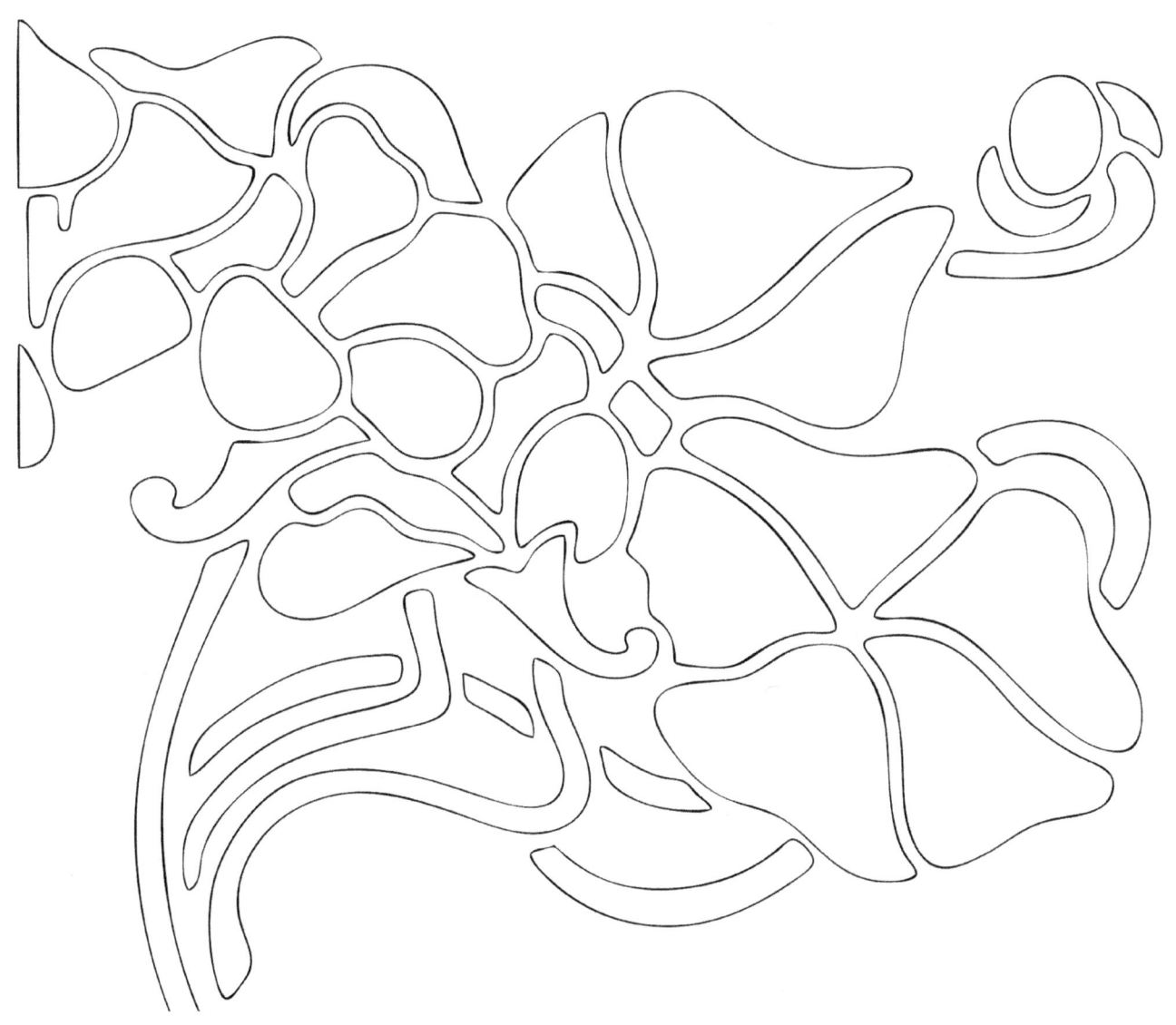

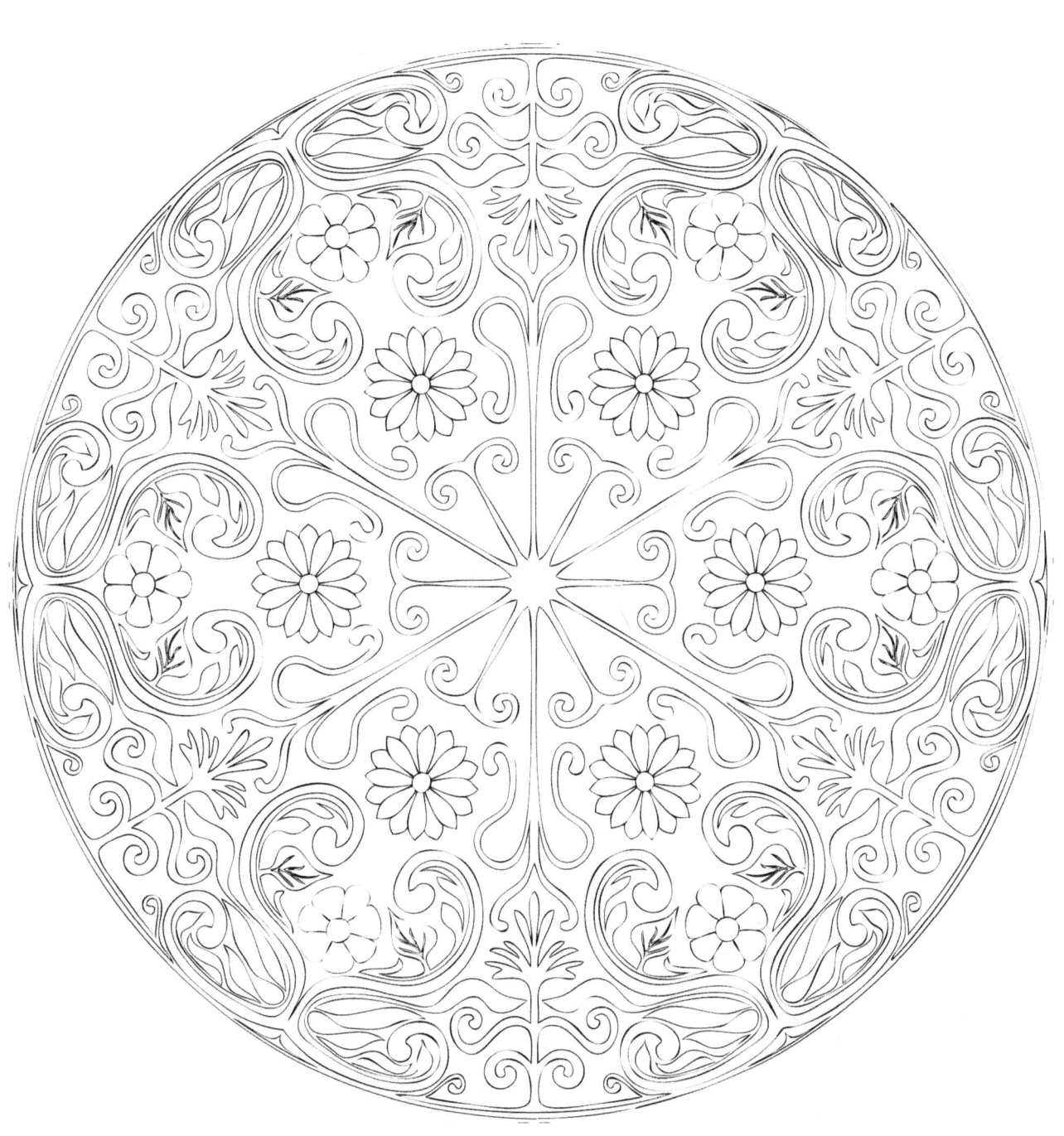

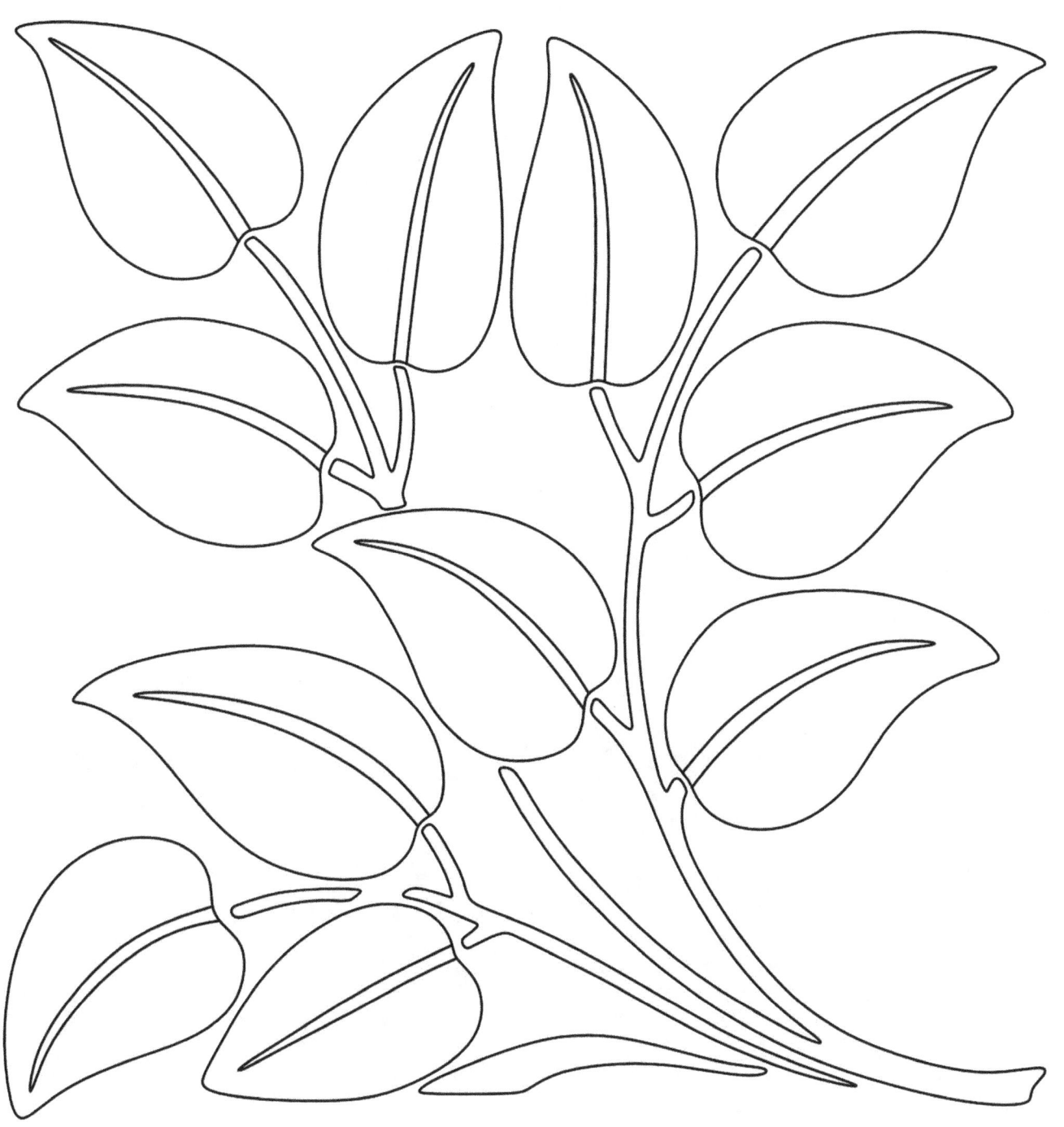

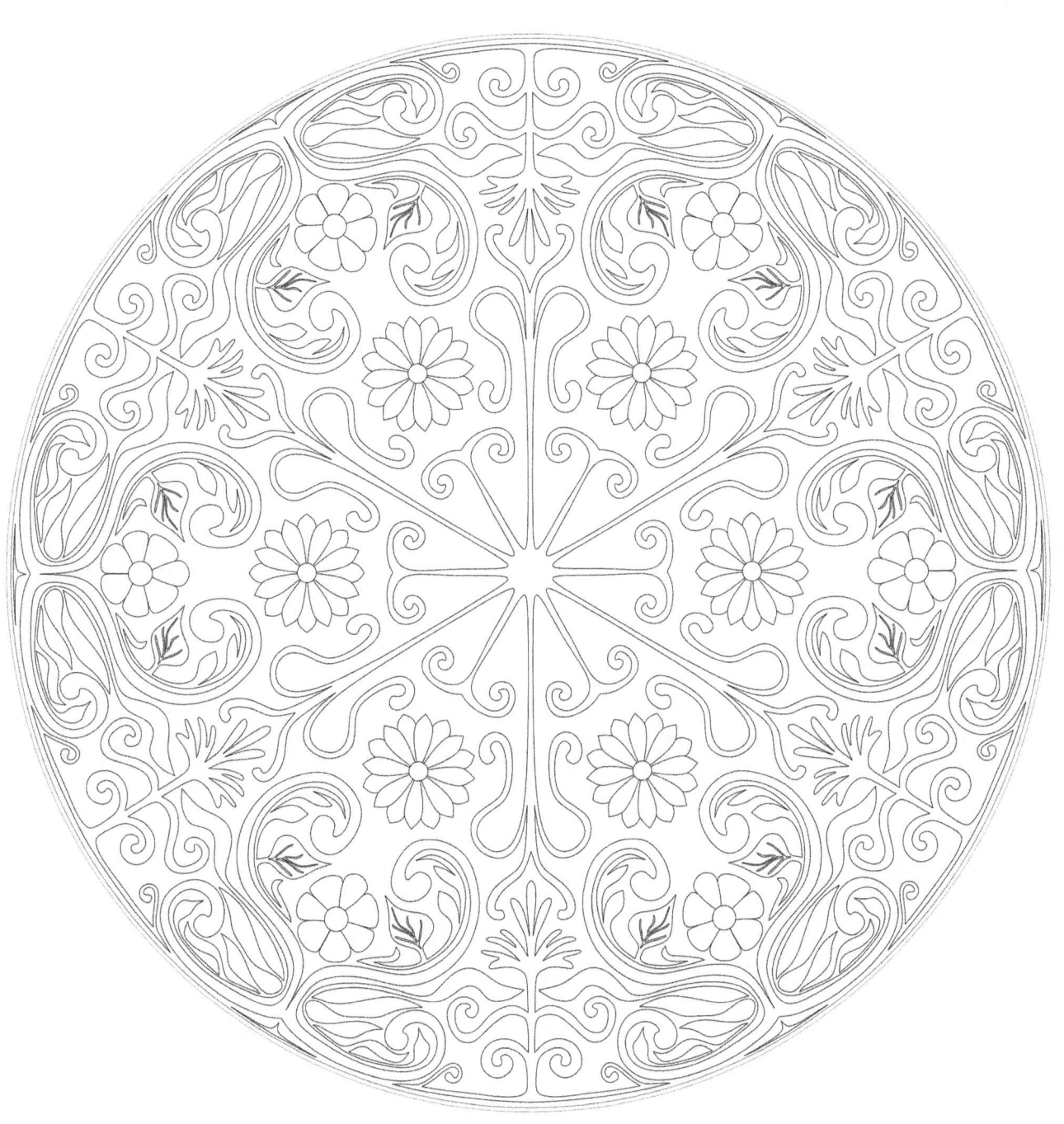

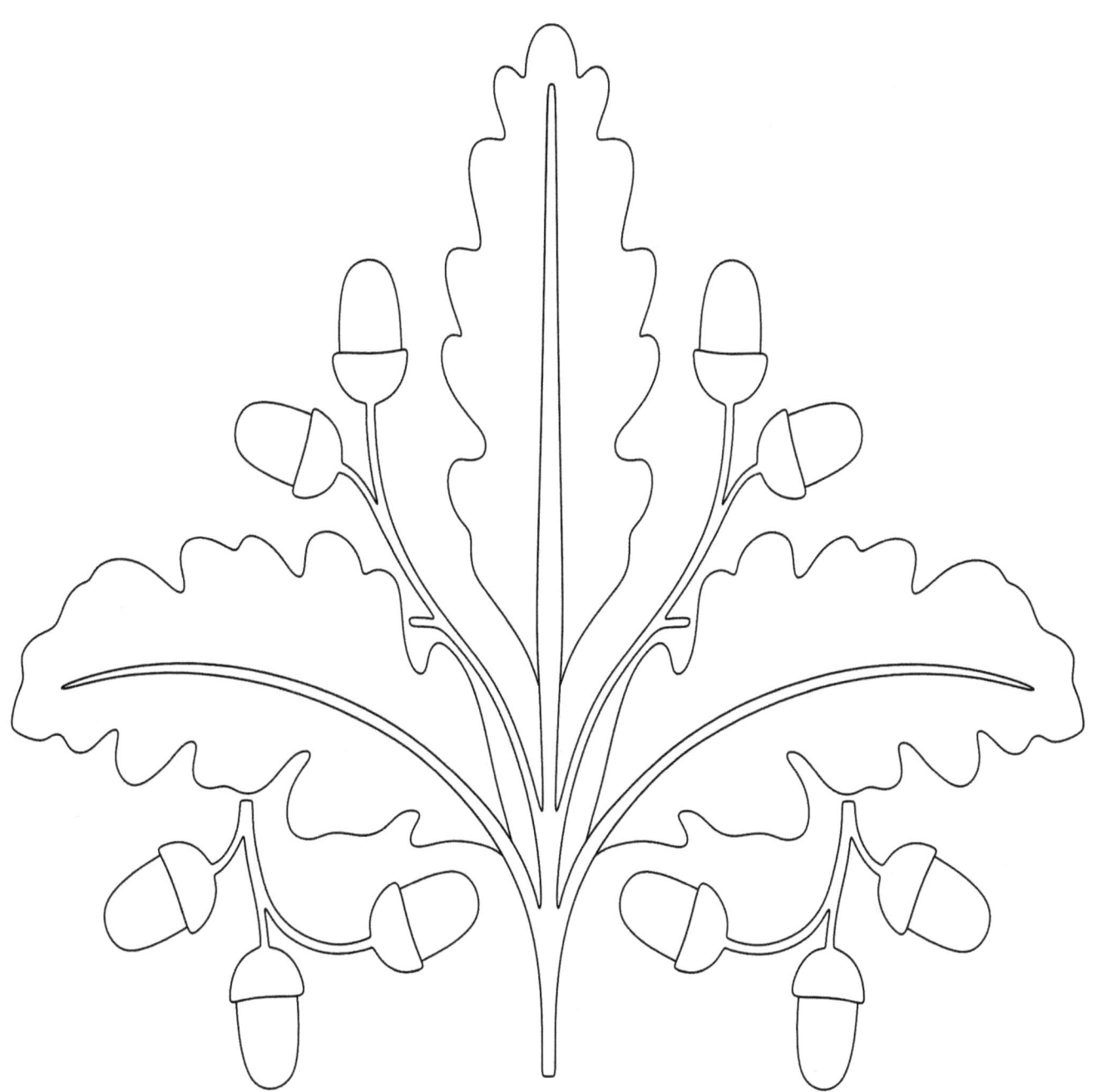

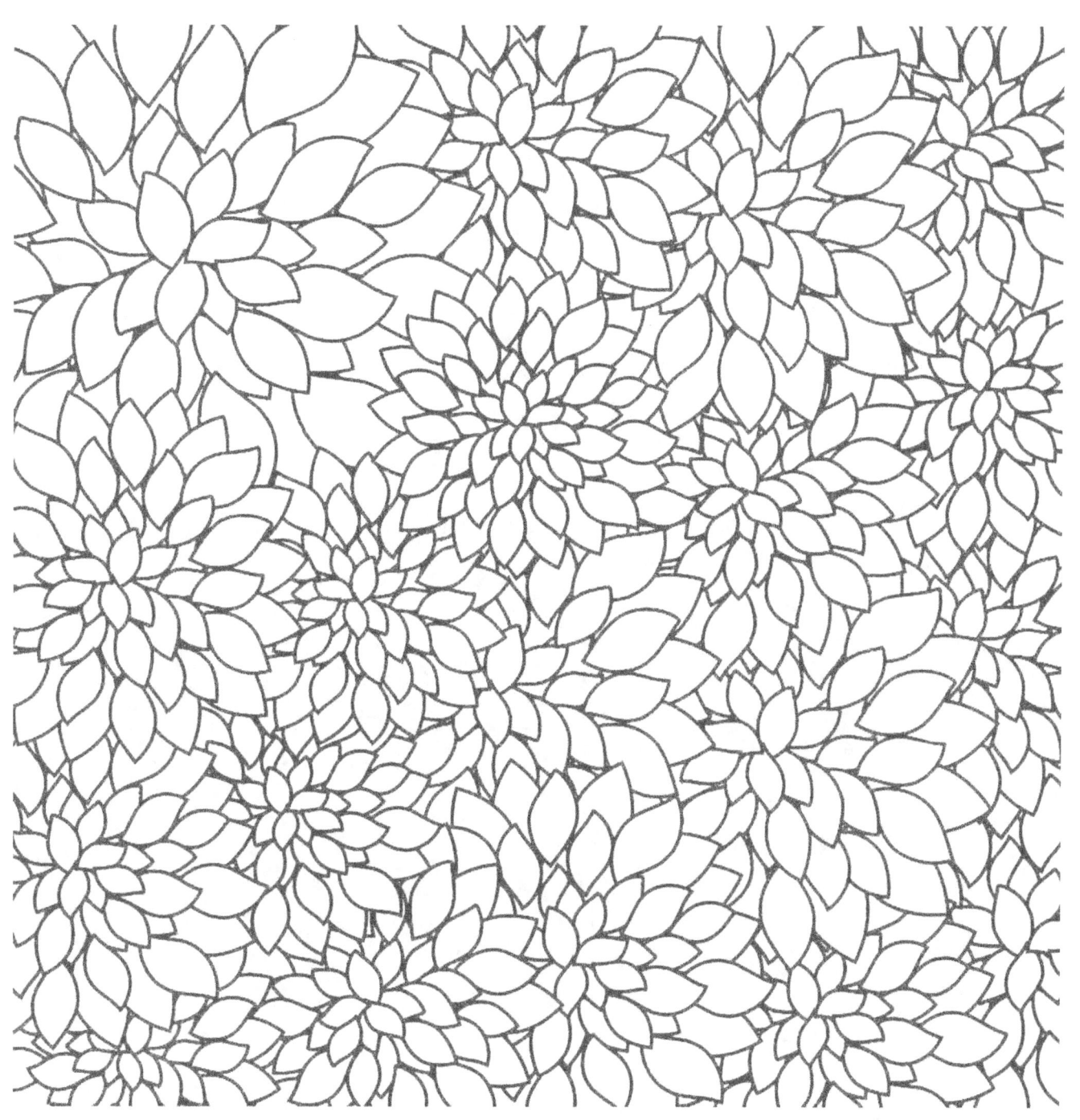

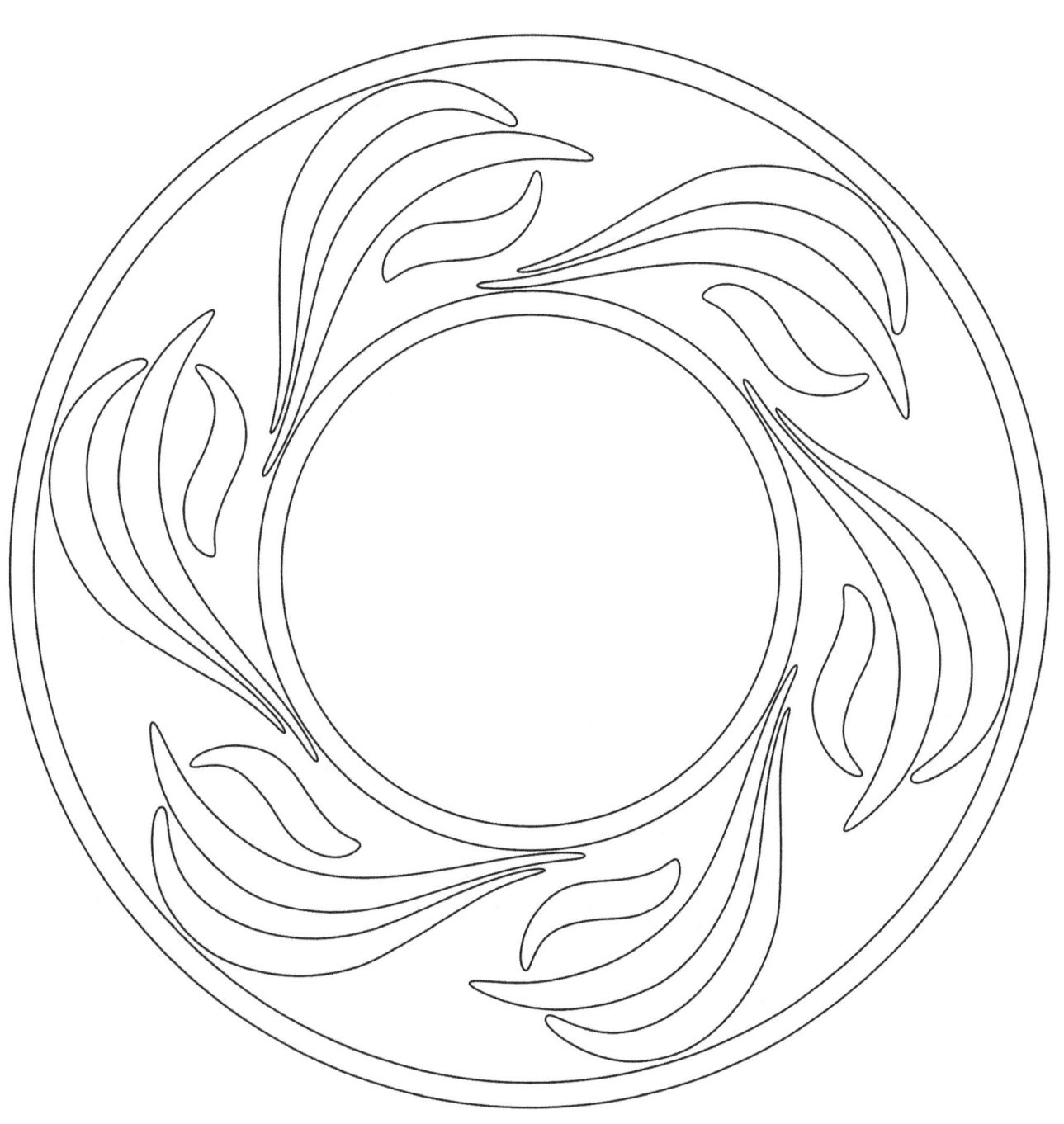

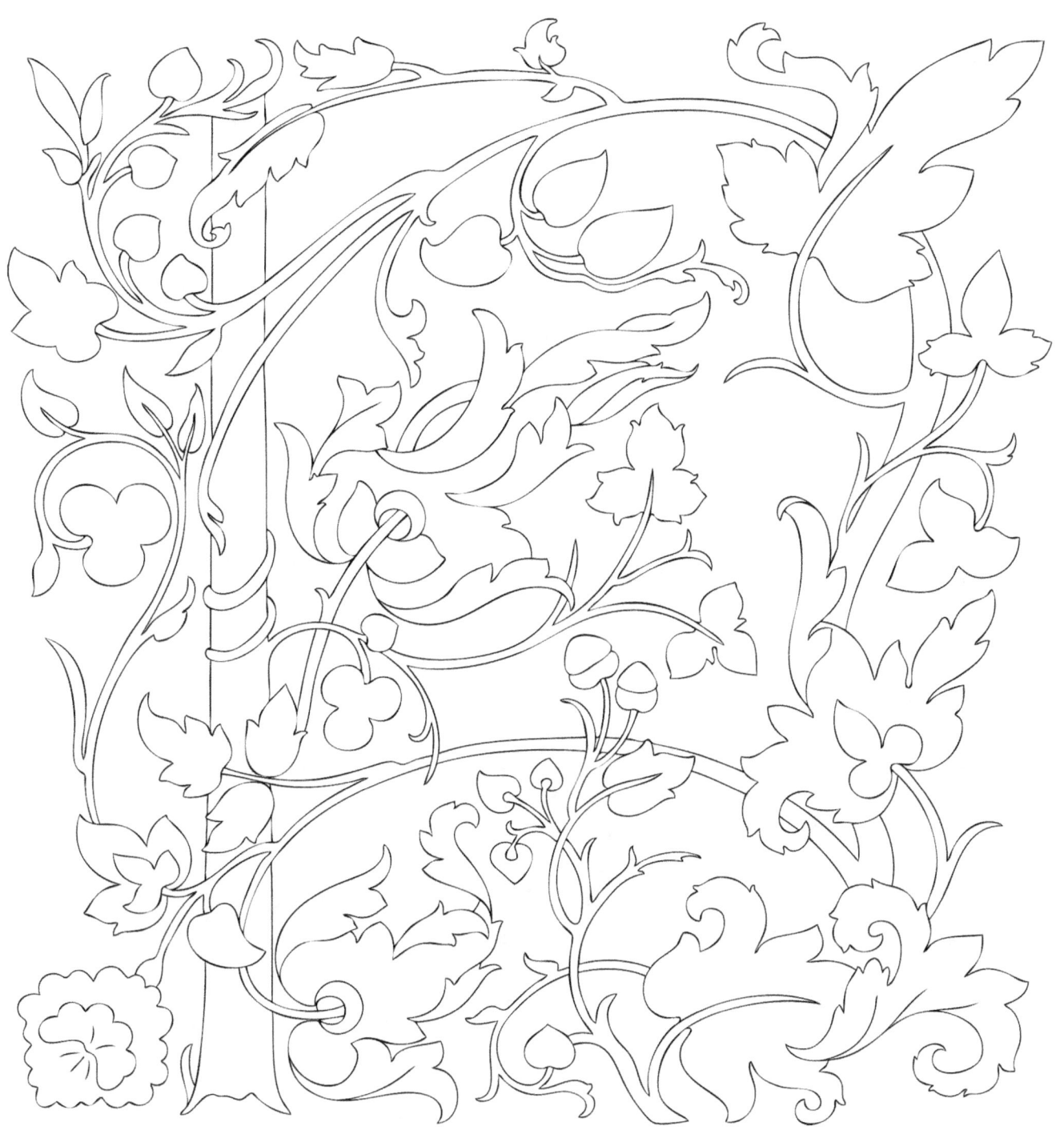

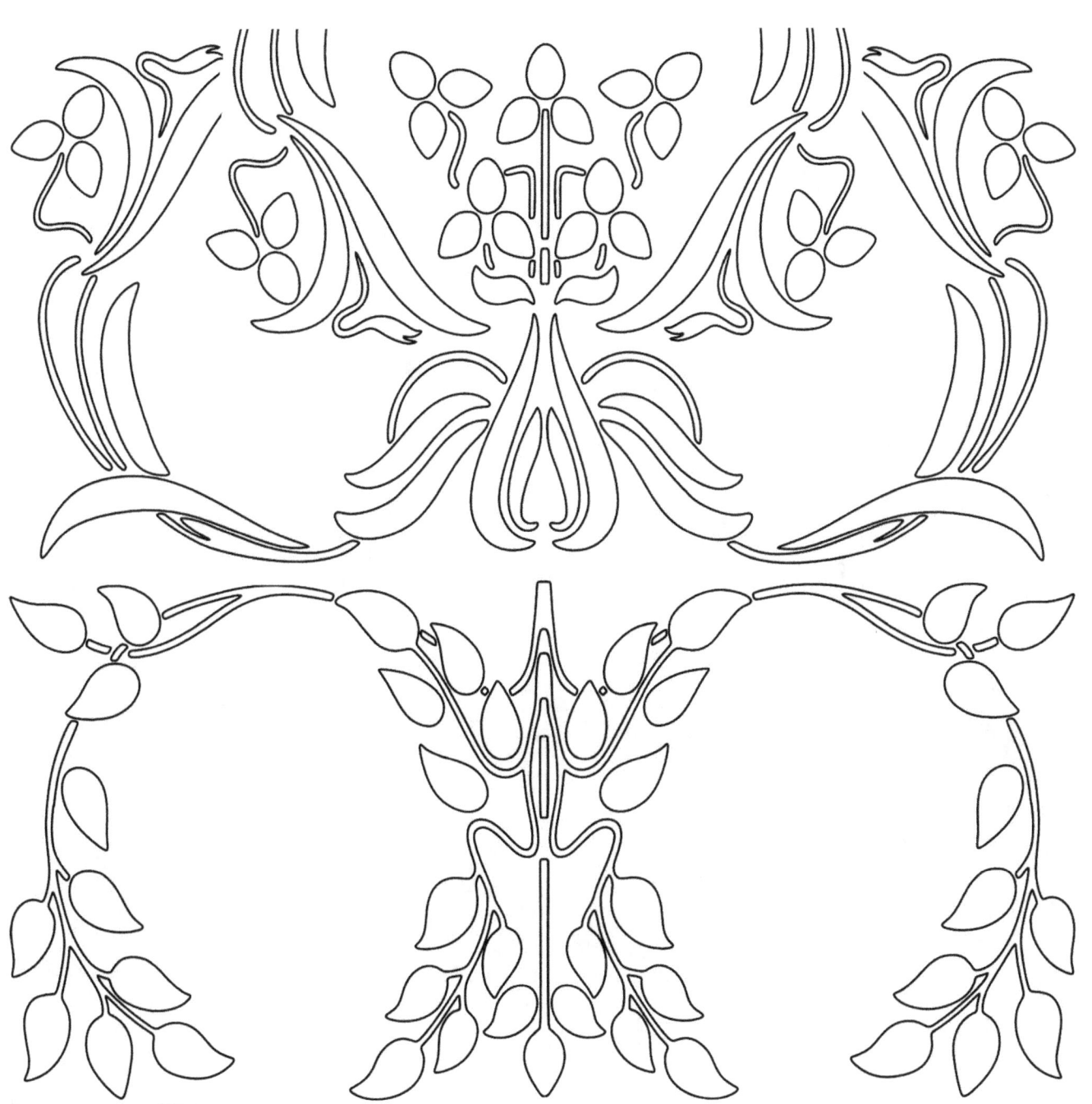

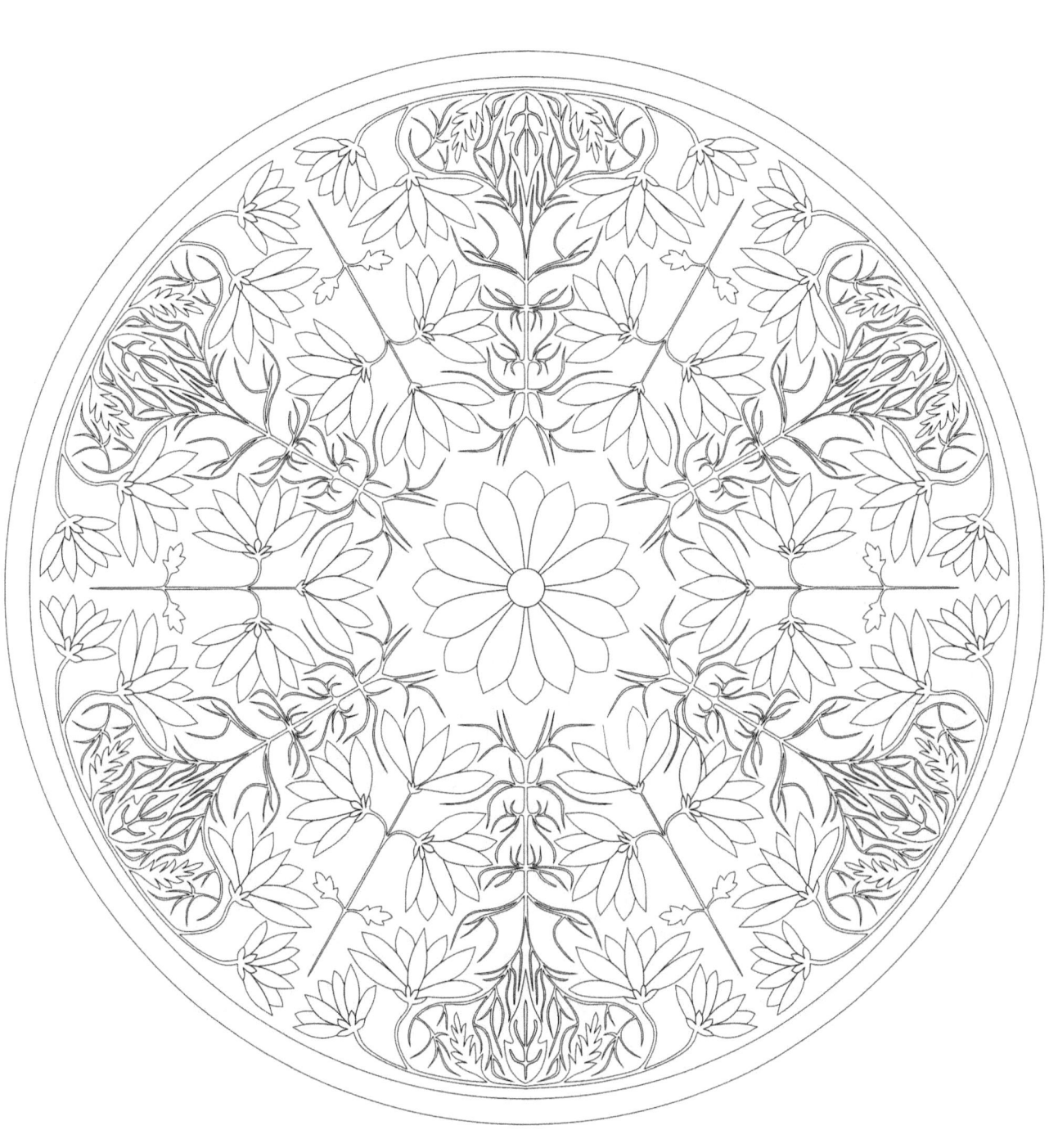

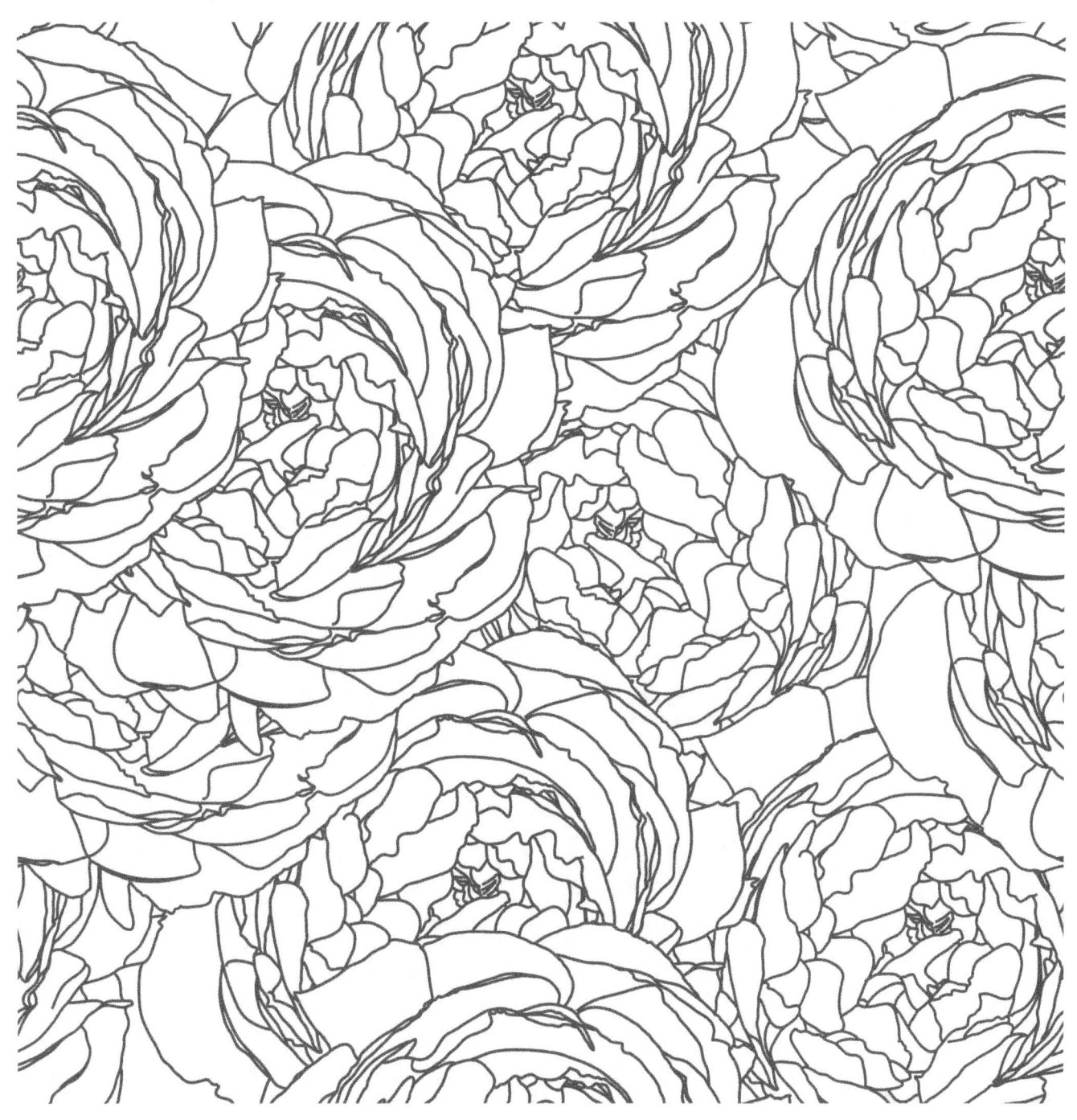

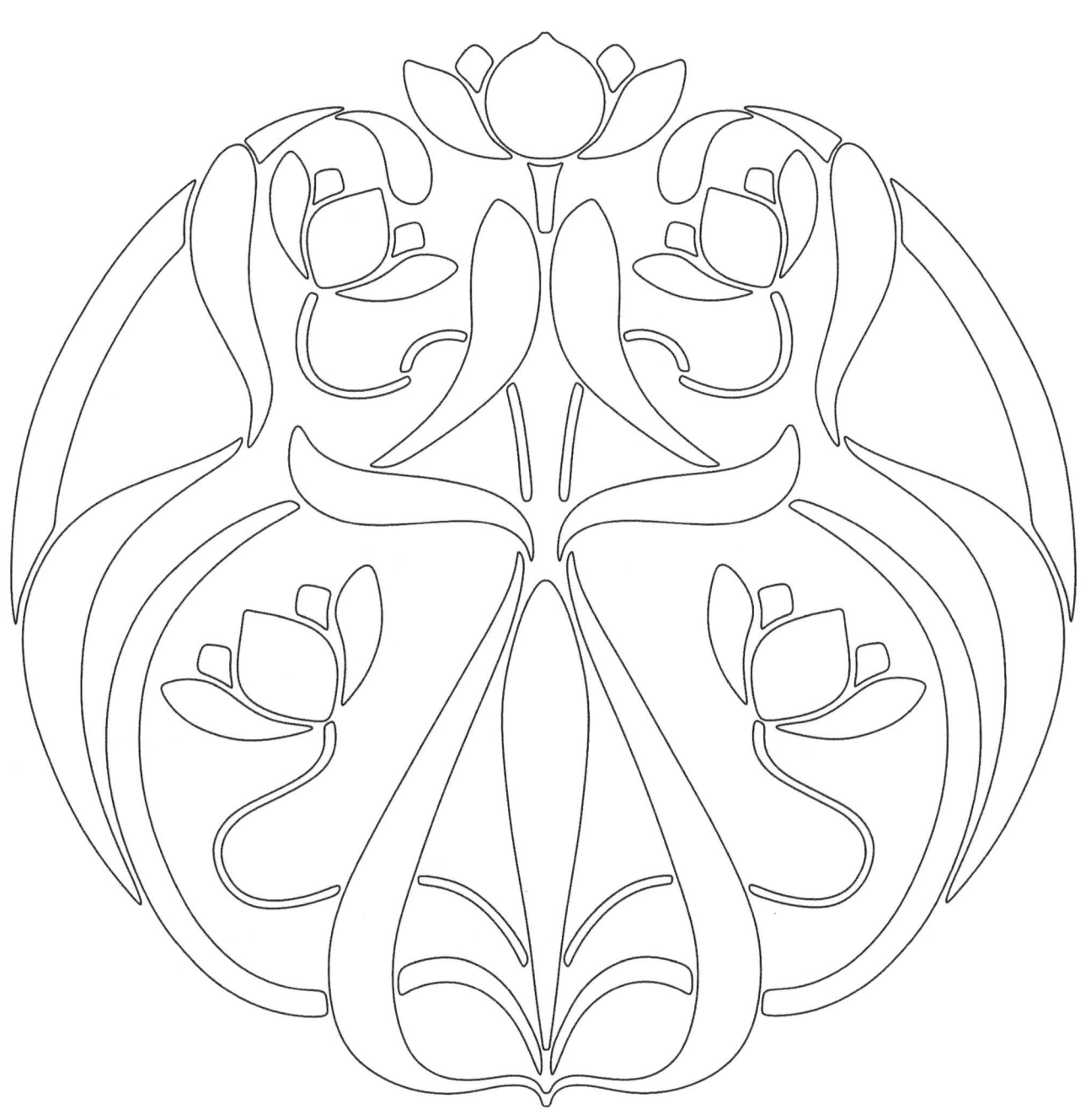

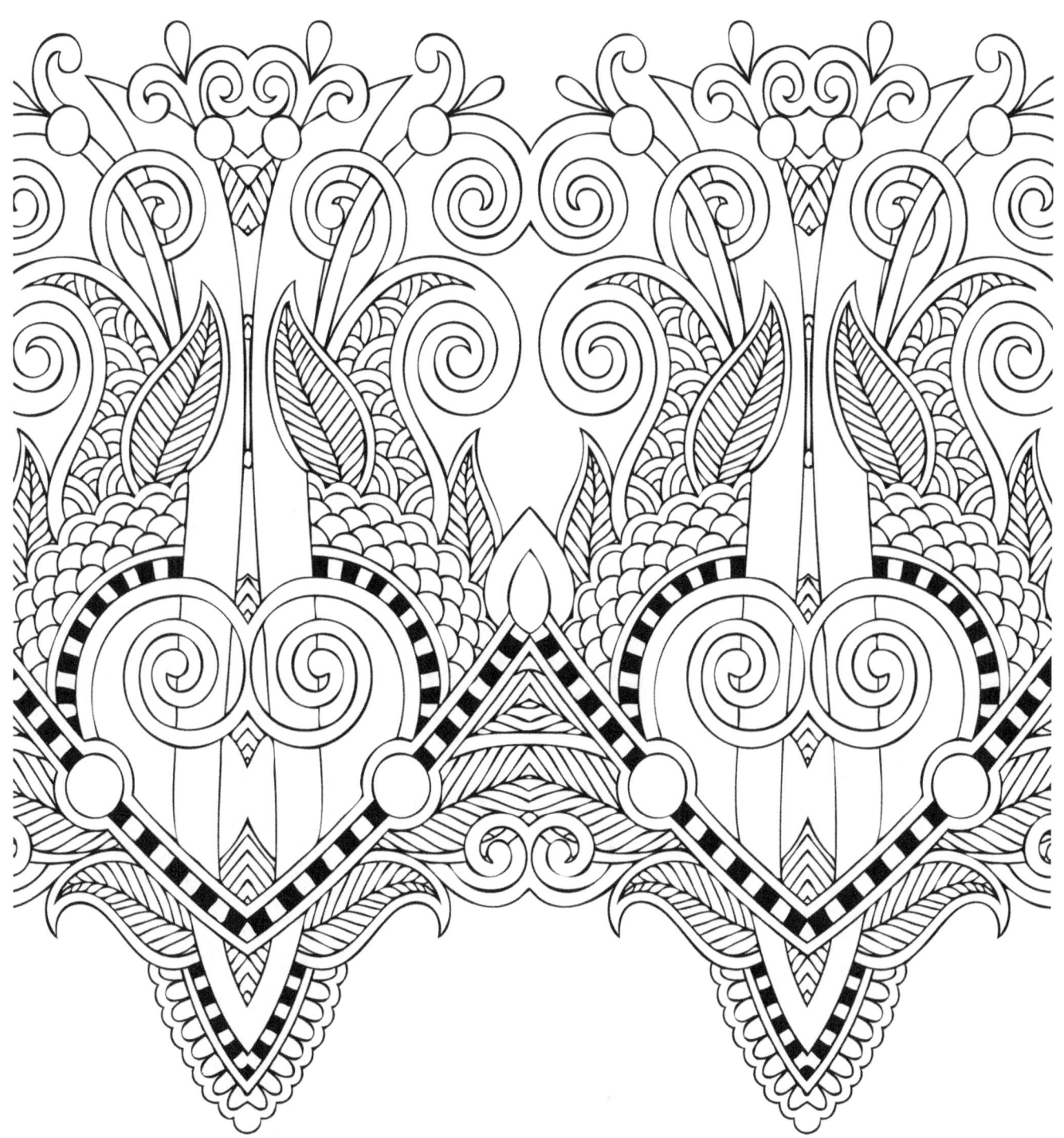

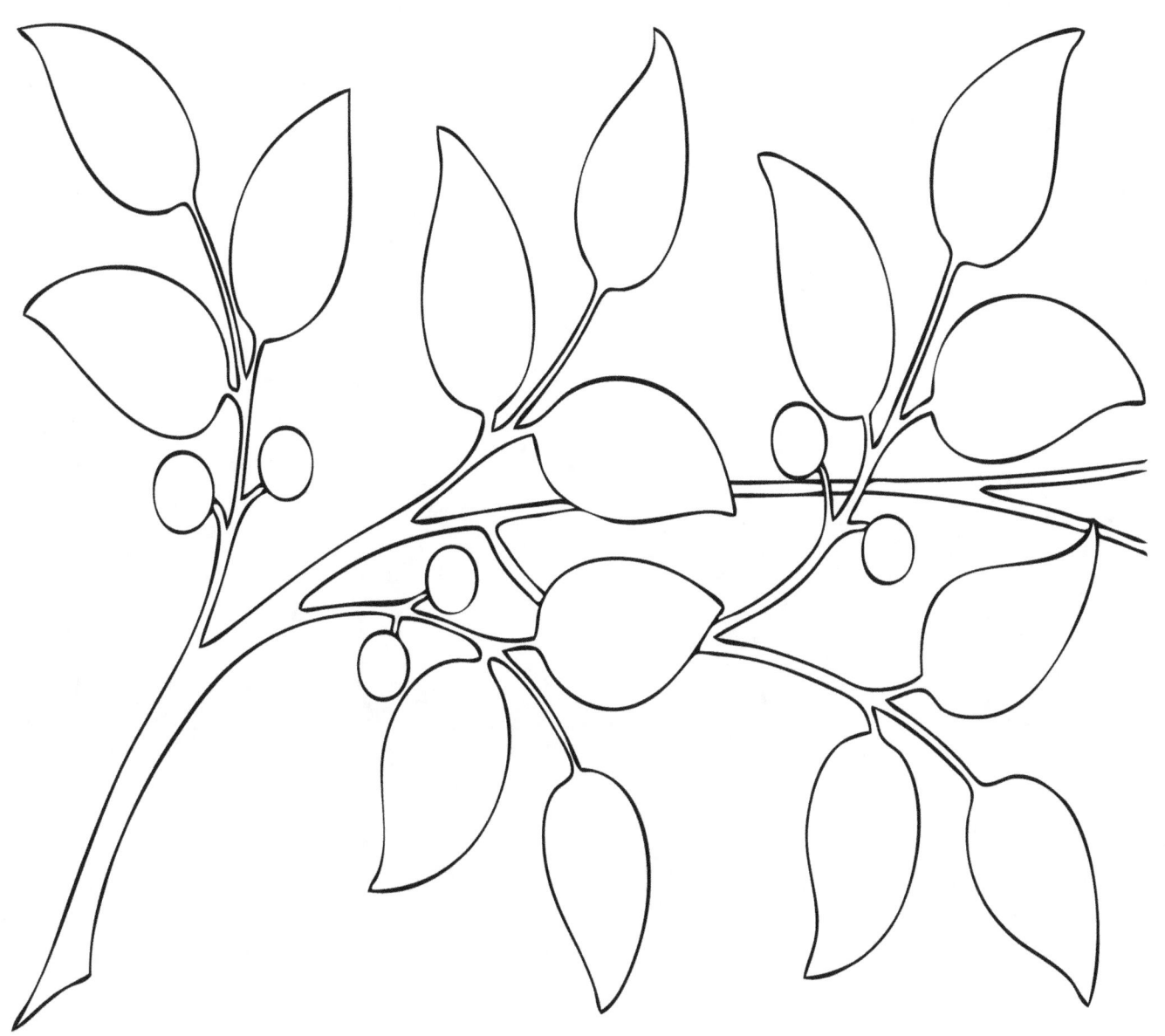

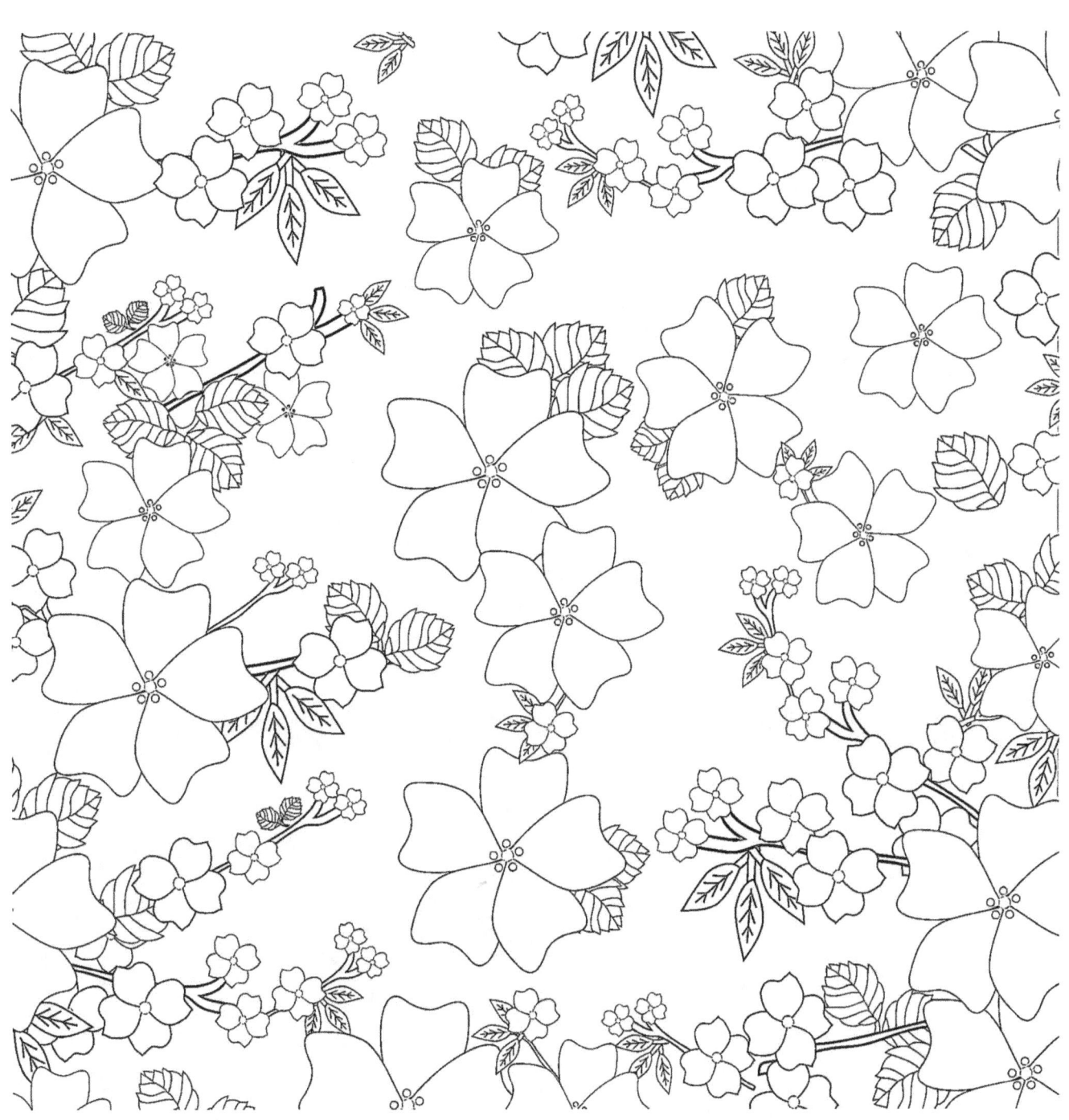

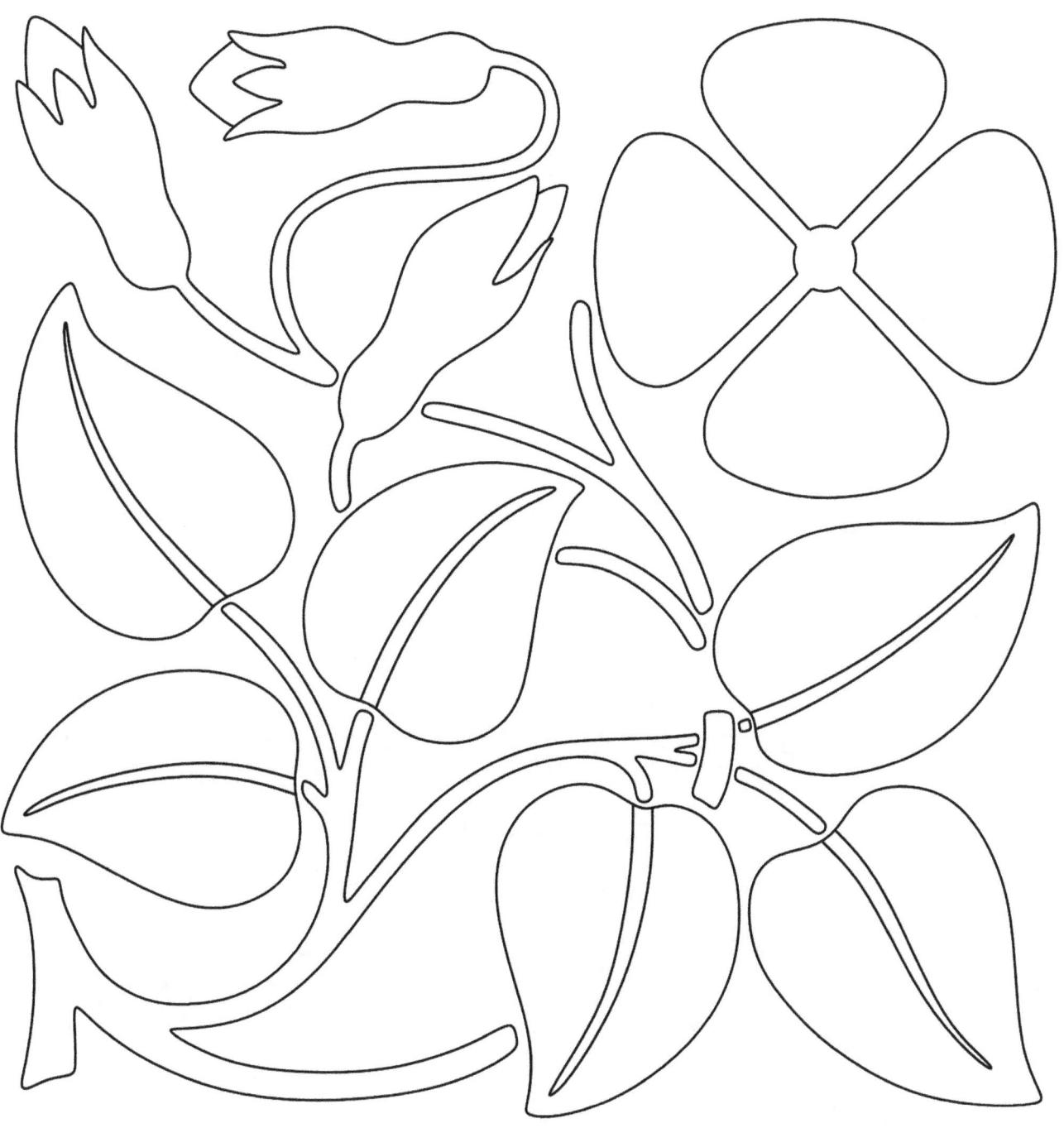

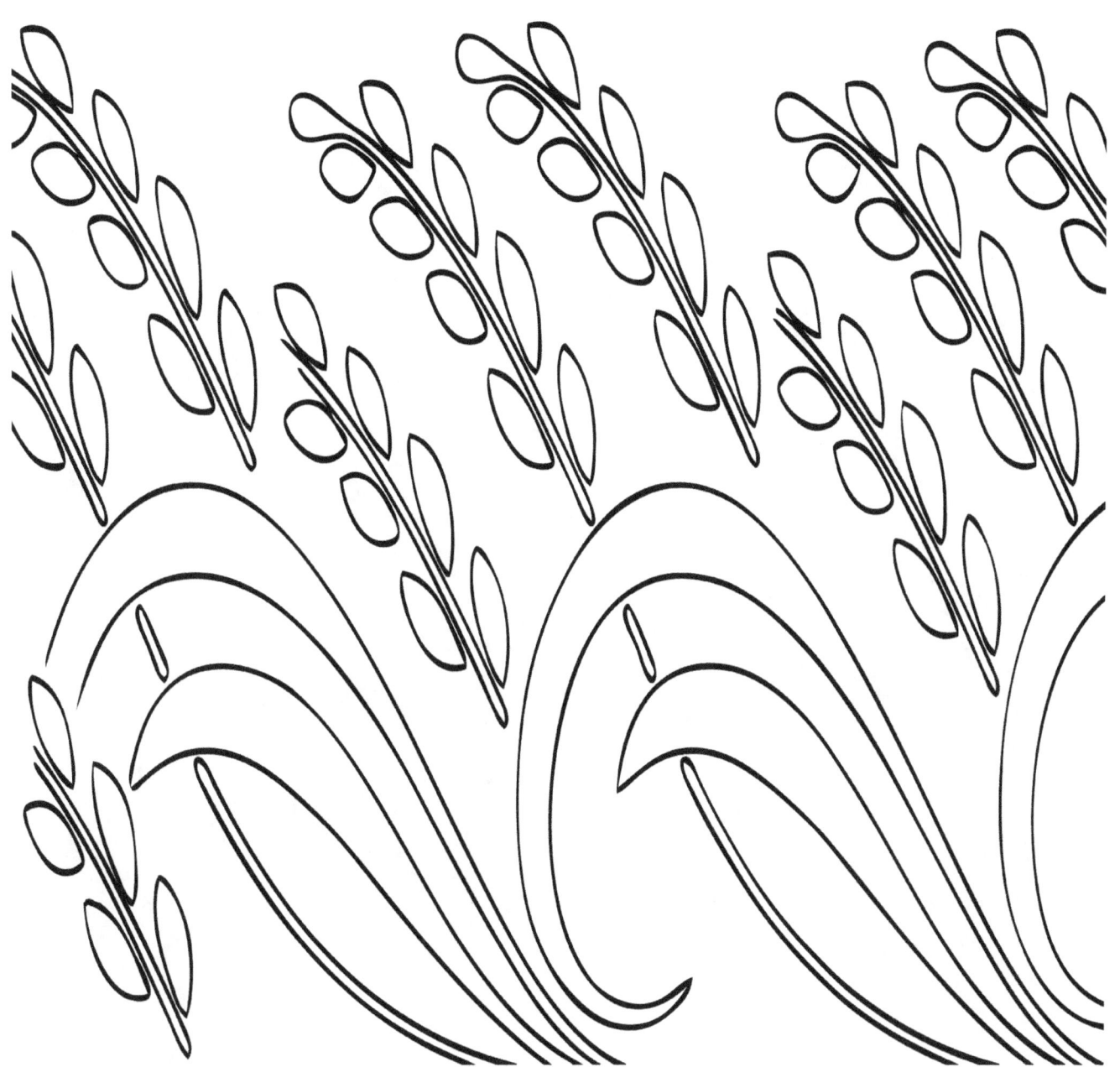

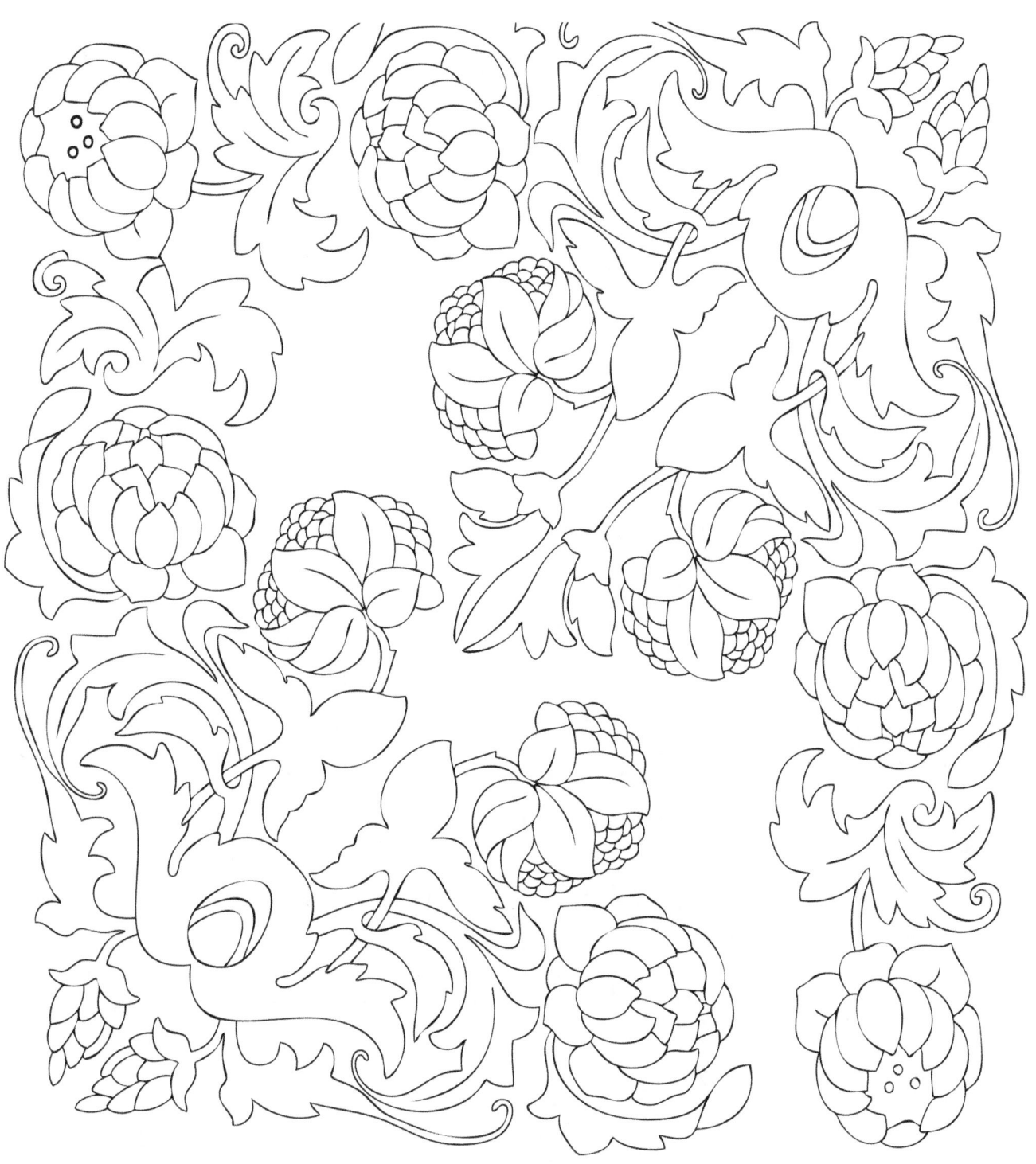

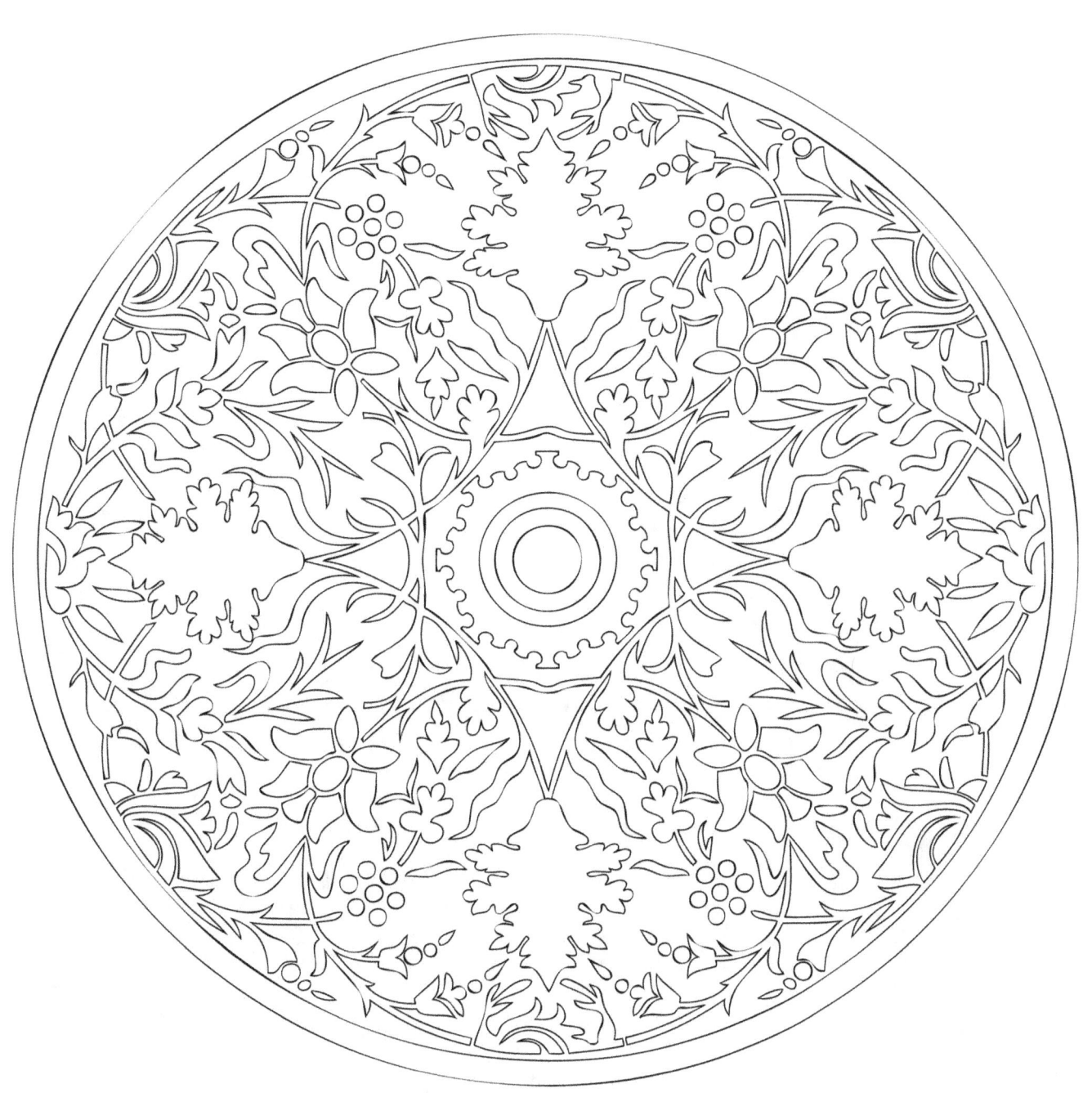

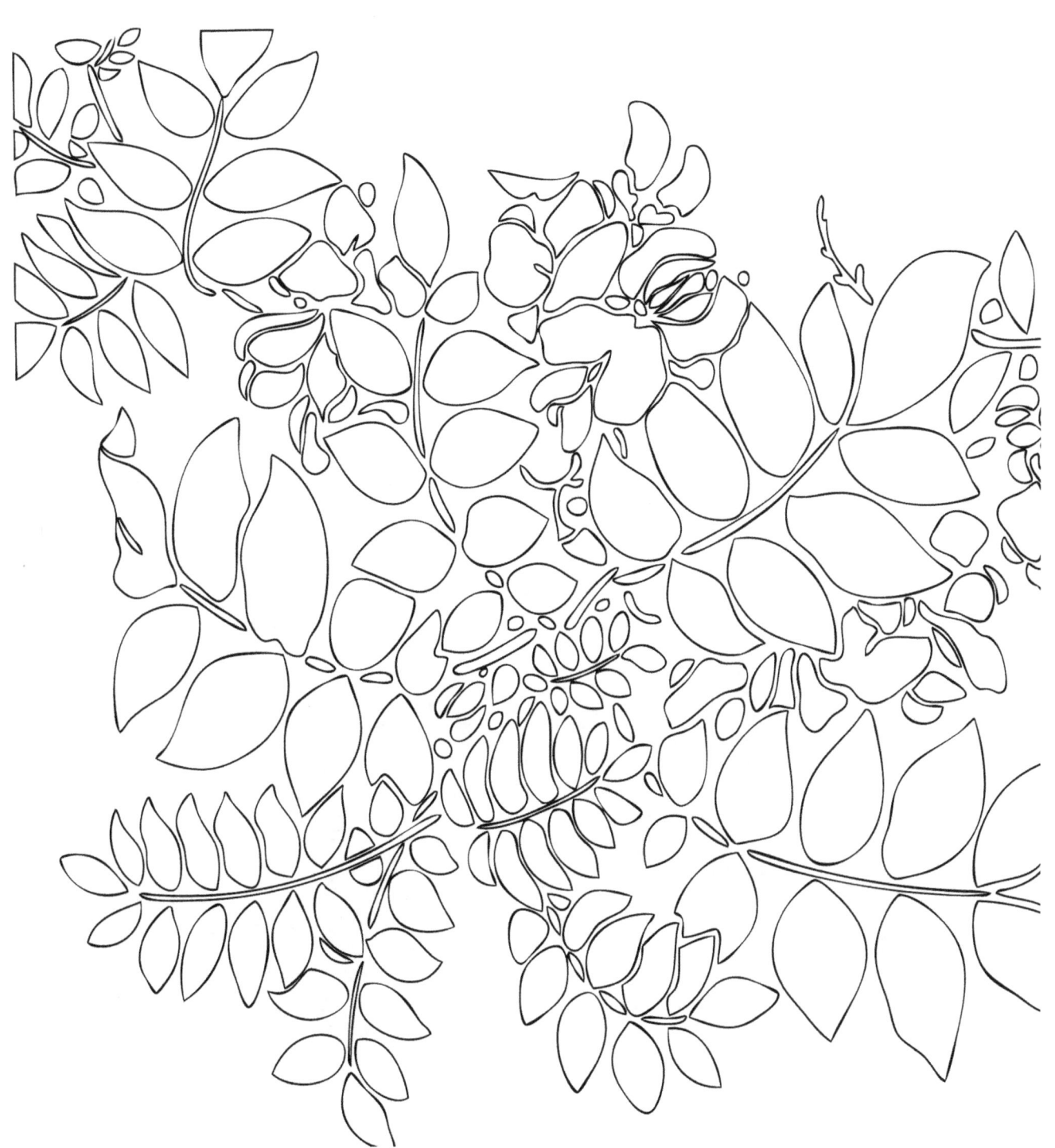

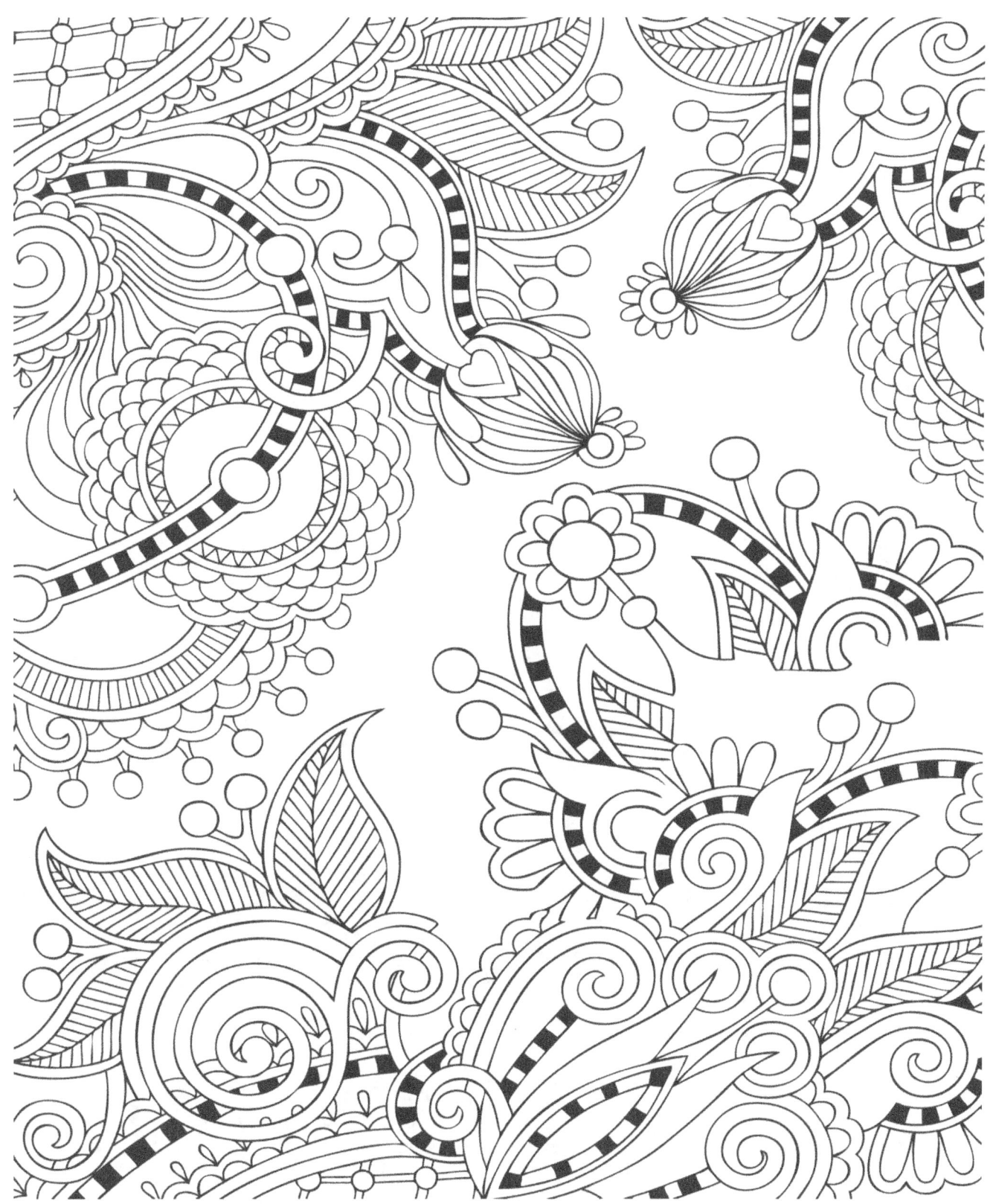

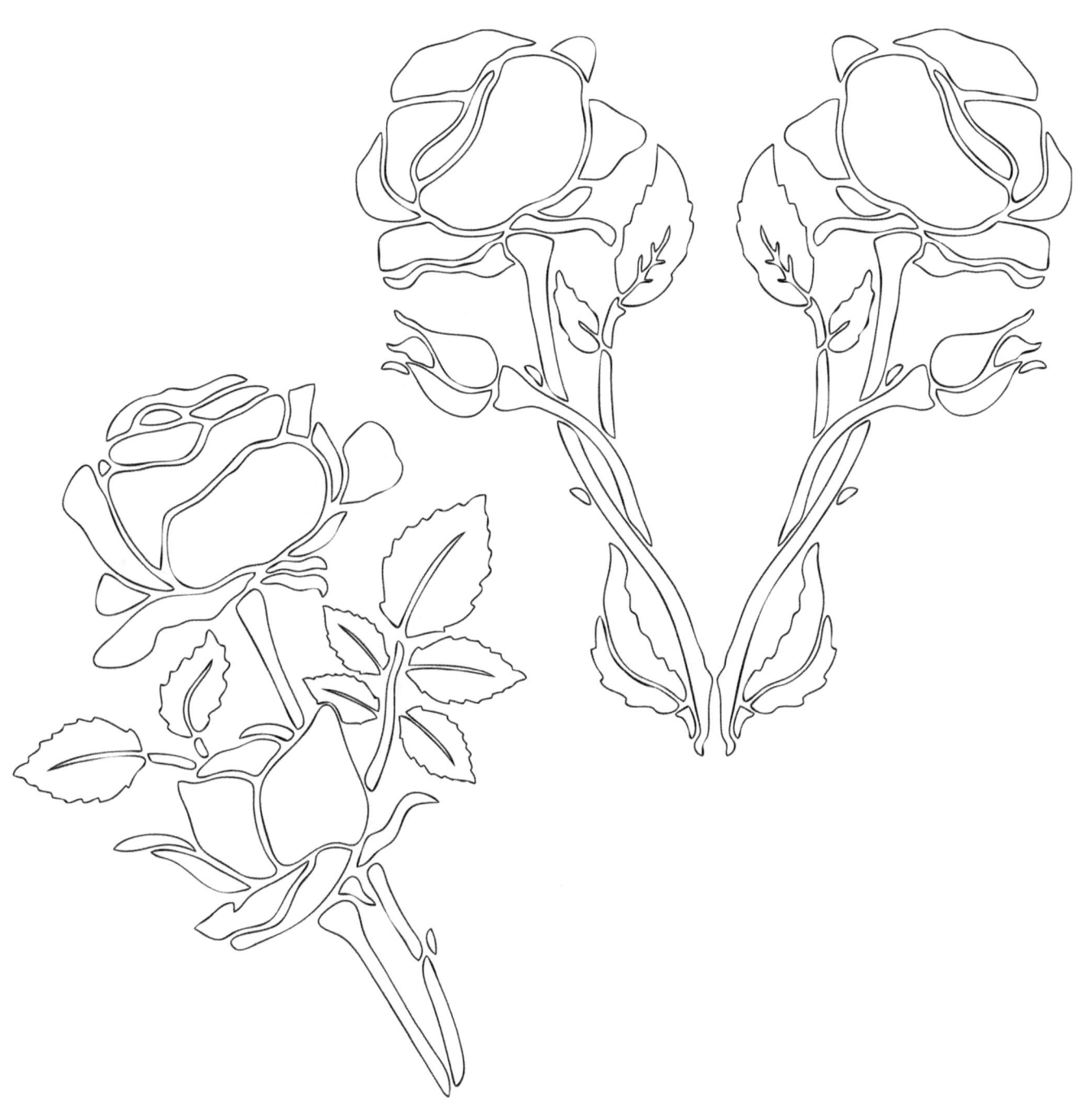

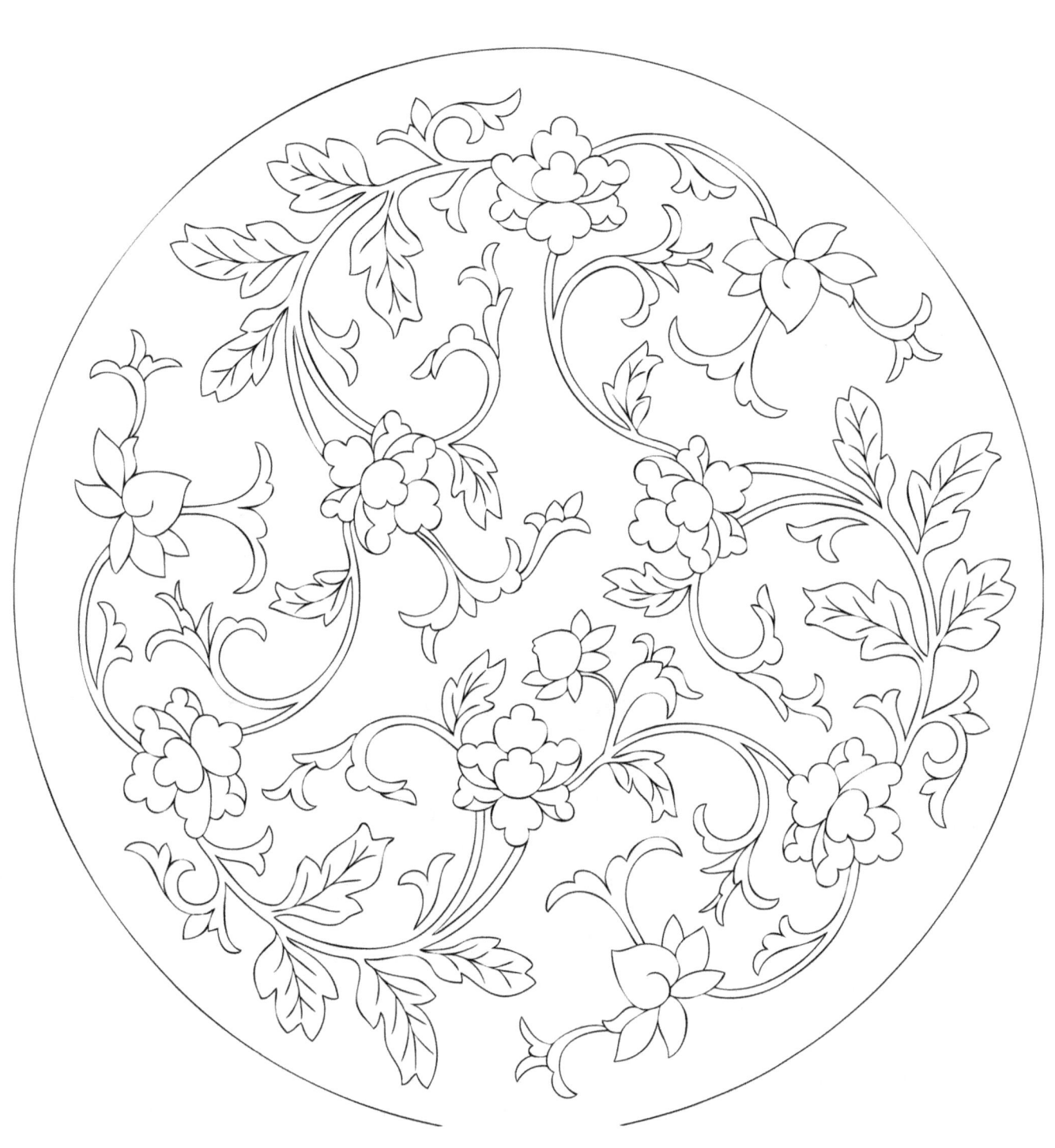

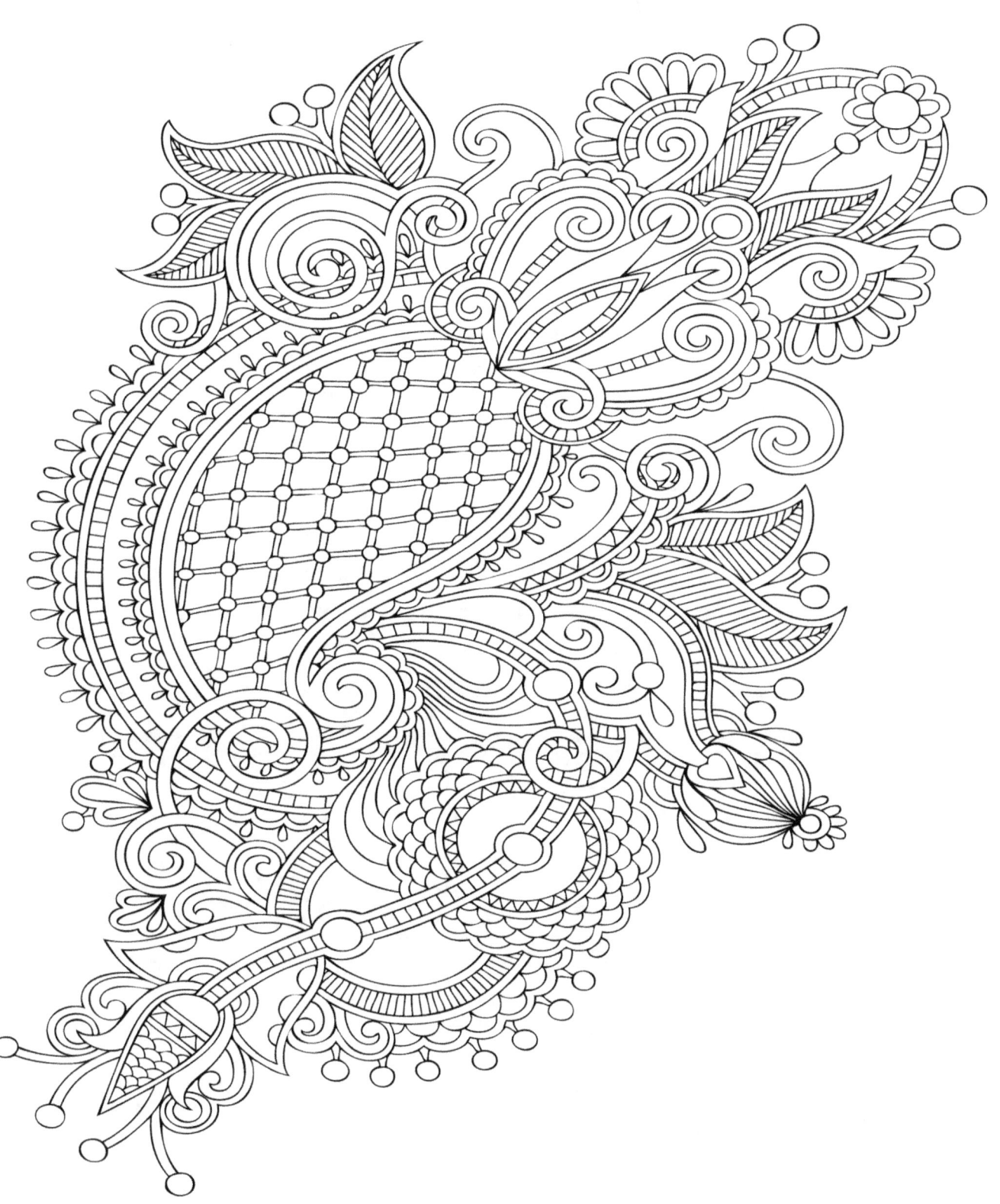

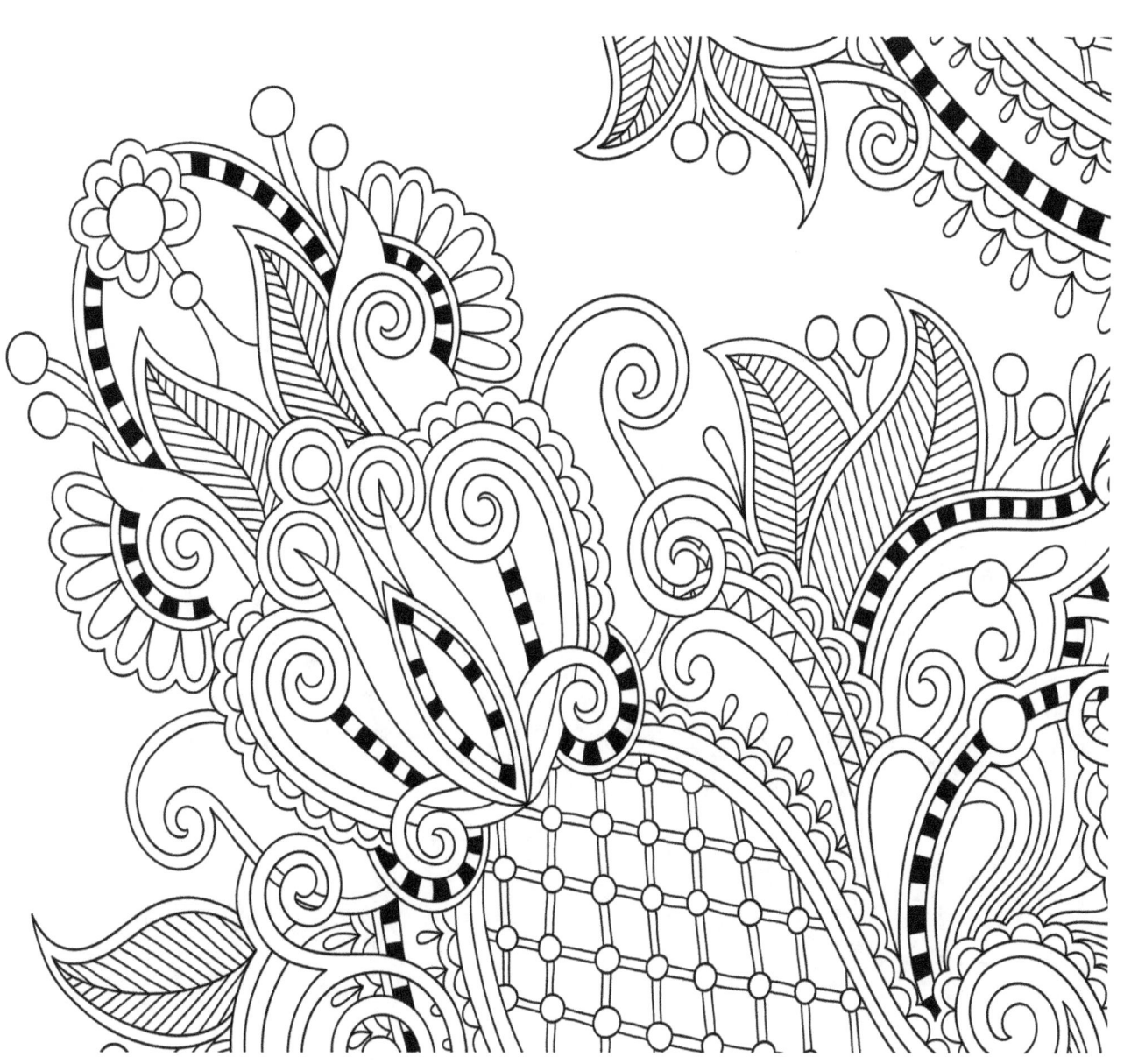

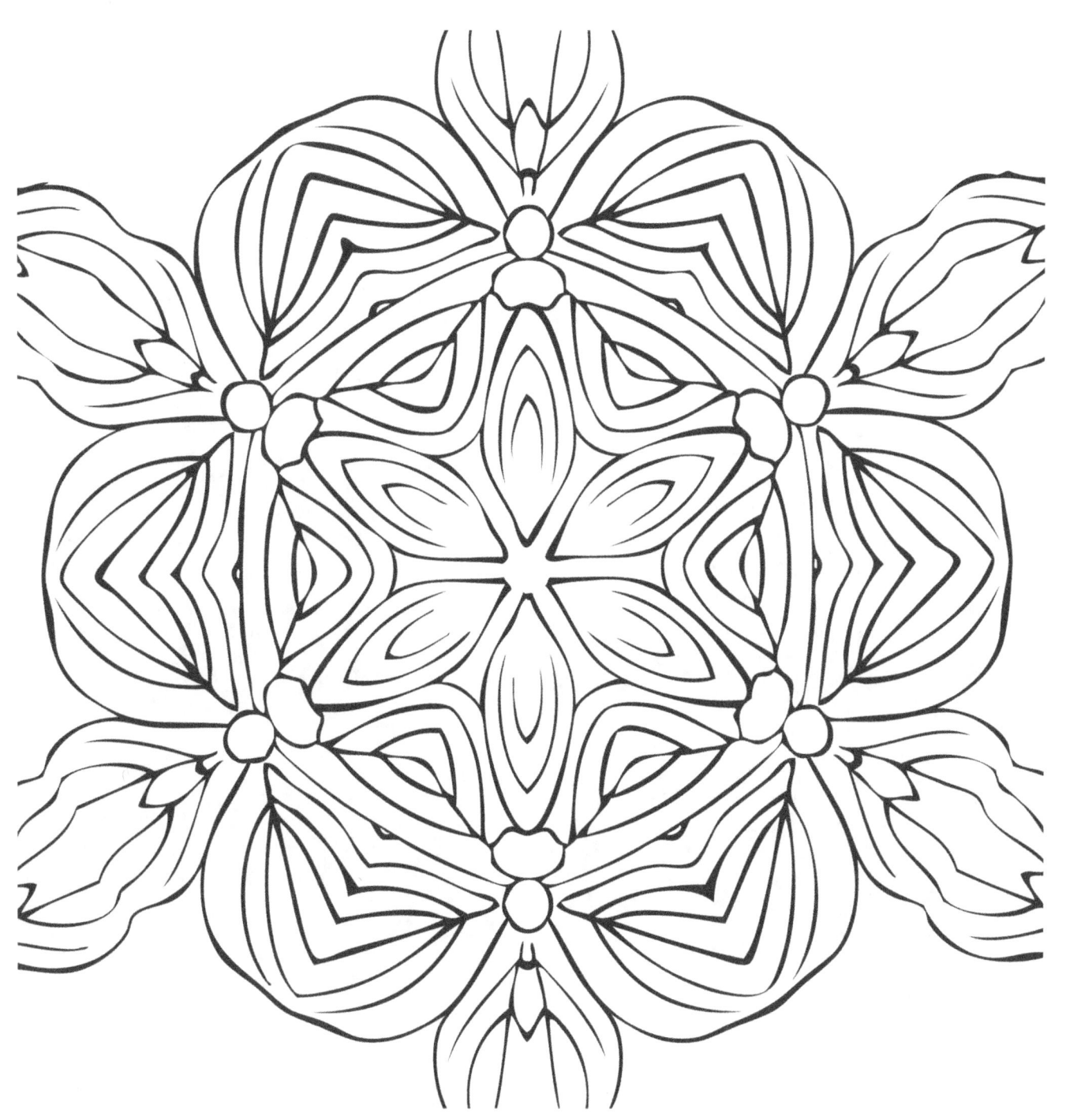

www.ingramcontent.com/pod-product-compliance
Lightning Source LLC
Chambersburg PA
CBHW080605180526
45168CB00007B/2791